PRINCEWILL LAGANG

Navigating Cultural Differences in Relationships

First published by PRINCEWILL LAGANG 2023

Copyright © 2023 by Princewill Lagang

All rights reserved. No part of this publication may be reproduced, stored or transmitted in any form or by any means, electronic, mechanical, photocopying, recording, scanning, or otherwise without written permission from the publisher. It is illegal to copy this book, post it to a website, or distribute it by any other means without permission.

Princewill Lagang asserts the moral right to be identified as the author of this work.

First edition

This book was professionally typeset on Reedsy.
Find out more at reedsy.com

Contents

1	Introduction	1
2	Cultural Awareness and Sensitivity	4
3	Embracing Diversity	7
4	Communication Across Cultures	10
5	Negotiating Traditions and Values	14
6	Family and Social Dynamics	18
7	Balancing Individual Identities	22
8	Overcoming Stereotypes and Misunderstandings	26
9	Navigating Celebrations and Holidays	30
10	Intercultural Parenting	34
11	Managing Conflicts and Challenges	38
12	Embracing the Journey	42

1

Introduction

In today's interconnected world, the dynamics of relationships have transcended geographical boundaries, resulting in an increasingly diverse tapestry of cultural backgrounds that intersect in personal and professional interactions. This chapter serves as an introduction to the multifaceted realm of cultural differences in relationships, delving into their significance, the challenges they pose, and the rewards they offer.

1.1 Significance of Cultural Differences in Relationships

Cultural differences, often manifested in varying norms, values, traditions, and communication styles, hold immense significance in the realm of relationships. They shape the way individuals perceive and interact with one another, influencing everything from romantic partnerships to friendships, family dynamics, and even workplace collaborations. Acknowledging and understanding these differences becomes paramount for fostering harmonious connections in a globalized society.

1.2 Challenges of Navigating Diverse Cultural Backgrounds

While cultural diversity enriches relationships, it also brings forth a set of challenges. Misunderstandings arising from differing cultural cues can lead to conflicts, misinterpretations, and a breakdown in effective communication. Stereotypes and preconceived notions often emerge as stumbling blocks, potentially hindering the genuine appreciation of each other's perspectives. Negotiating these challenges requires open-mindedness, patience, and a willingness to learn and adapt.

1.3 Rewards of Embracing Cultural Diversity

Amidst the challenges lie remarkable rewards for those who embrace cultural diversity in relationships. Exposure to different worldviews expands one's horizons, promoting personal growth and empathy. Collaborations between individuals from diverse backgrounds can lead to innovative solutions and creative outcomes, enriched by the amalgamation of varied insights. Furthermore, the ability to navigate cultural differences successfully fosters a deep sense of connection and respect, forming the foundation of lasting and meaningful relationships.

1.4 Structure of the Book

This book is structured to provide a comprehensive exploration of cultural differences in relationships. Following this introduction, each subsequent chapter will delve into specific aspects of cultural diversity, including communication patterns, conflict resolution, familial expectations, and romantic relationships. Through a combination of research findings, real-life anecdotes, and practical advice, readers will gain a holistic understanding of how to navigate and thrive within the intricate landscape of culturally diverse relationships.

In summary, this chapter sets the stage for a thought-provoking journey into the realm of cultural differences in relationships. By highlighting their significance and examining the challenges and rewards they entail, we lay

INTRODUCTION

the groundwork for an in-depth exploration of how individuals can navigate, appreciate, and flourish within the tapestry of human connections that spans the globe.

2

Cultural Awareness and Sensitivity

In a world marked by diverse cultural landscapes, cultivating a heightened sense of cultural awareness and sensitivity becomes instrumental in fostering meaningful relationships. This chapter delves into the significance of understanding and respecting each other's cultural backgrounds, elucidating how cultural awareness enhances communication, deepens connections, and paves the way for harmonious interactions.

2.1 The Significance of Understanding Cultural Backgrounds

At the heart of cultural awareness lies the profound significance of comprehending and valuing the intricacies of each other's cultural backgrounds. Recognizing the historical, social, and religious underpinnings that shape individuals' perspectives and behaviors cultivates a climate of respect and empathy. By appreciating the diversity that cultural backgrounds bring to relationships, individuals are better equipped to navigate potential pitfalls and engage in constructive dialogue.

2.2 Enhancing Communication through Cultural Awareness

Effective communication is the bedrock of any successful relationship, and cultural awareness plays a pivotal role in this realm. Acknowledging cultural nuances in verbal and nonverbal communication helps avoid misunderstandings and misinterpretations. An understanding of different communication styles, such as direct versus indirect expression, can prevent unintentional offense and promote smoother interactions. Through the lens of cultural awareness, individuals gain the tools to communicate with sensitivity, active listening, and genuine interest.

2.3 Deepening Connections through Respectful Engagement

Cultural sensitivity is not just about avoiding misunderstandings; it is about embracing differences with an open heart. By displaying respect for diverse customs, traditions, and values, individuals can forge connections that transcend superficial boundaries. Respectful engagement involves actively seeking to learn about and appreciate the uniqueness of each other's cultural identities. This kind of engagement not only enriches relationships but also fosters a sense of belonging and acceptance.

2.4 Navigating Challenges with Cultural Sensitivity

Cultural differences may occasionally give rise to conflicts or challenges. However, a foundation of cultural sensitivity equips individuals to navigate these moments with grace and understanding. Rather than approaching disagreements with a judgmental mindset, individuals can draw from their cultural awareness to delve into the root causes of conflicts and address them in a constructive manner. This approach fosters reconciliation and growth within relationships.

2.5 Empathy as a Cornerstone of Cultural Sensitivity

At the core of cultural awareness and sensitivity lies the ability to empathize with experiences and perspectives different from one's own. Empathy fosters a genuine connection by allowing individuals to step into each other's shoes, understand the influences that shape behaviors, and relate on a human level. Through empathy, relationships transcend the surface and enter a realm of depth and authenticity.

In conclusion, Chapter 2 emphasizes the pivotal role of cultural awareness and sensitivity in nurturing relationships. By understanding the significance of cultural backgrounds, enhancing communication, deepening connections, and approaching challenges with empathy, individuals can build bridges that span cultural divides. This chapter lays the groundwork for the subsequent exploration of practical strategies and insights that empower individuals to navigate the complexities of culturally diverse relationships with finesse and compassion.

3

Embracing Diversity

Diversity, in all its forms, presents a unique opportunity for growth and enrichment within relationships. This chapter delves into the myriad benefits of diversity in relationships, highlighting how cultural differences can serve as catalysts for personal development, mutual understanding, and the evolution of deeper connections.

3.1 The Power of Diversity in Relationships

Diversity, encompassing differences in cultural backgrounds, experiences, perspectives, and identities, has the potential to invigorate relationships. Rather than being obstacles, these differences can be sources of strength. By embracing diversity, individuals introduce a multitude of insights and approaches that can lead to innovative solutions, creative collaborations, and a broader worldview.

3.2 Cultural Differences as Pathways to Personal Growth

Navigating relationships with individuals from different cultural backgrounds presents an opportunity for profound personal growth. Exposure to new ways of thinking challenges preconceived notions and encourages self-reflection. The discomfort that may arise from encountering unfamiliar customs fosters adaptability and open-mindedness. This journey of personal growth not only enhances one's emotional intelligence but also cultivates a sense of resilience and flexibility.

3.3 Fostering Mutual Understanding through Cultural Differences

Cultural differences offer a gateway to enhanced mutual understanding. Engaging in conversations about each other's backgrounds promotes a deeper awareness of the forces that have shaped one's perspectives and values. As individuals share stories of their cultural heritage, they invite their counterparts to glimpse into their world, forming bridges of empathy. This process dissolves stereotypes, diminishes biases, and paves the way for a richer connection built on genuine appreciation.

3.4 Strengthening Bonds through Shared Learning

Embracing diversity encourages a shared journey of learning and discovery. As individuals explore each other's cultures, they gain insights into rituals, traditions, celebrations, and histories that extend beyond their own experiences. This process of shared learning fosters a sense of intimacy, as both parties invest in understanding and valuing each other's identities. This willingness to engage with curiosity strengthens the bonds between individuals.

3.5 Cultivating an Inclusive Mindset

An inclusive mindset is the cornerstone of embracing diversity. It involves acknowledging that every individual's perspective is shaped by their unique cultural background. By actively seeking out diverse viewpoints and experiences, individuals enrich their own understanding of the world. This mindset encourages individuals to celebrate differences and actively create an environment where all voices are heard and valued.

In conclusion, Chapter 3 underscores the transformative potential of embracing diversity within relationships. By recognizing the benefits of diversity, fostering personal growth through cultural differences, nurturing mutual understanding, and cultivating an inclusive mindset, individuals can tap into a wellspring of shared wisdom and forge connections that are both authentic and resilient. The subsequent chapters will delve into practical strategies to harness the power of diversity and cultivate relationships that thrive on the strength of their differences.

4

Communication Across Cultures

Effective communication is the linchpin of successful relationships, particularly when navigating diverse cultural backgrounds. This chapter delves into the intricate ways cultural nuances impact communication styles and offers practical strategies to facilitate meaningful and productive cross-cultural interactions.

4.1 Cultural Nuances: Shaping Communication Styles

Communication is more than words; it's a complex interplay of verbal and nonverbal cues deeply influenced by cultural contexts. Different cultures prioritize elements such as directness, indirectness, context, and hierarchy in communication. These nuances can lead to misunderstandings or misinterpretations if not recognized and respected.

4.2 The Impact of High-Context and Low-Context Cultures

Cultures can be broadly categorized into high-context and low-context communication styles. High-context cultures rely on implicit communication, where much is conveyed through context, tone, and nonverbal cues. Low-context cultures, on the other hand, prioritize explicit and direct communication. Understanding this dichotomy helps individuals navigate conversations more adeptly.

4.3 Strategies for Effective Cross-Cultural Communication

1. Active Listening: Paying close attention to both verbal and nonverbal cues helps capture the intended meaning behind words.

2. Cultural Humility: Approach conversations with humility, acknowledging that your perspective is just one among many valid viewpoints.

3. Clarification: Don't hesitate to seek clarification if something is unclear. Paraphrasing what you've understood ensures accuracy.

4. Avoiding Assumptions: Challenge assumptions about communication norms. What's acceptable in one culture might be perceived differently in another.

5. Respectful Inquiry: Ask open-ended questions to encourage deeper explanations and insights into the cultural context.

6. Adapting Language: Adjust your language to accommodate varying levels of language proficiency among interlocutors.

4.4 Nonverbal Communication and Body Language

Nonverbal cues can vary significantly across cultures. Gestures, facial expressions, eye contact, and personal space all hold distinct meanings. Recognizing and adapting to these cues is crucial for avoiding unintended offense or miscommunication.

4.5 Bridging Communication Gaps

When communication gaps arise due to cultural differences, take proactive steps to bridge them:

1. Cultural Education: Invest time in learning about the cultural norms and communication styles of the individuals you interact with.

2. Feedback Loop: Encourage open dialogue and feedback to address any misunderstandings promptly.

3. Patience and Empathy: Be patient with the process of understanding and be empathetic toward the challenges of cross-cultural communication.

4. Building Rapport: Establishing rapport and trust can mitigate misunderstandings and facilitate smoother communication.

4.6 Technology and Virtual Communication

In an increasingly globalized world, virtual communication is common. However, cultural cues can be more challenging to pick up online. To bridge this gap, consider video calls to observe facial expressions and body language, and be aware of potential time zone differences that may affect communication.

In conclusion, Chapter 4 highlights the intricate interplay of cultural nuances in communication and the strategies that enable effective cross-cultural interactions. By recognizing the impact of high-context and low-context cultures, practicing active listening, adapting communication styles, and fostering cultural humility, individuals can communicate across cultural divides with respect, clarity, and empathy. The subsequent chapters will continue to build on these foundations, offering insights into conflict resolution, intimacy, and sustainable relationships in culturally diverse contexts.

5

Negotiating Traditions and Values

As relationships traverse cultural boundaries, they encounter the intersections of diverse traditions, values, and beliefs. This chapter delves into the art of navigating these differences, providing insights into how individuals can respect each other's backgrounds while finding common ground and avenues for compromise.

5.1 Acknowledging the Significance of Traditions and Values

Traditions and values are the tapestries woven from cultural histories and personal experiences. Acknowledging their importance lays the groundwork for productive discussions and respectful negotiations.

5.2 The Complexities of Cultural Traditions

Cultural traditions can encompass a wide spectrum, from rituals and celebrations to familial roles and societal expectations. These traditions hold deep meaning and often contribute to an individual's sense of identity and belonging.

5.3 Navigating Value Differences with Sensitivity

Values, rooted in cultural and personal beliefs, guide individuals' decision-making and priorities. Clashes in values can lead to conflicts if not addressed constructively.

5.4 Approaches for Finding Common Ground

1. Open Dialogue: Initiate candid conversations about traditions and values to understand their significance to each other.

2. Shared Values: Identify shared values that can serve as foundations for mutual understanding.

3. Compromise: Seek middle ground that respects both parties' values and allows for a harmonious coexistence.

4. Selective Incorporation: Integrate aspects of each other's traditions into daily life or special occasions.

5. Education: Educate each other about the historical, social, or religious context of specific traditions to foster empathy and understanding.

5.5 Balancing Individual and Collective Needs

When traditions or values clash, individuals must balance their personal needs with the needs of the relationship. This might involve finding ways to preserve certain traditions while adapting others to align with shared goals.

5.6 Honoring Both Sides: Avoiding Token Gestures

While compromise is essential, avoid treating traditions as mere tokens. Genuine respect requires understanding and appreciating the depth behind each tradition or value.

5.7 Navigating Family Expectations

Families often have expectations regarding traditions and values. Honest communication with families, highlighting the significance of your relationship, can lead to understanding and support.

5.8 Embracing Hybrid Identities

In some cases, individuals from different cultural backgrounds might adopt a hybrid identity that draws from both traditions. Embracing this identity can offer a unique way to navigate diverse values.

5.9 Recognizing Deal-Breakers

While compromise is crucial, there might be values or traditions that are non-negotiable for either party. These instances require careful consideration and discussion about the relationship's future.

5.10 Continuous Adaptation

Relationships evolve, and so can the negotiation of traditions and values. Flexibility and a willingness to adapt as circumstances change are essential for sustainable relationships.

In conclusion, Chapter 5 dives into the intricacies of negotiating traditions and values in culturally diverse relationships. By acknowledging the significance of traditions and values, fostering open dialogue, seeking common ground, and maintaining sensitivity to individual and collective needs, individuals can navigate these complex waters with respect and understanding. This chapter serves as a cornerstone for the subsequent exploration of conflict resolution, intimacy, and long-term relationship sustainability within the context of diverse cultural backgrounds.

6

Family and Social Dynamics

The impact of cultural diversity extends beyond individuals to encompass their families and the broader social context. This chapter delves into the complex role of extended families and societal norms in cross-cultural relationships, providing insights into navigating family expectations while nurturing the relationship itself.

6.1 The Intricacies of Extended Families

In many cultures, family extends beyond nuclear units to encompass extended relatives. The influence of extended family members can significantly shape relationship dynamics and decisions.

6.2 The Intersection of Social Norms

Societal norms, influenced by cultural heritage, play a crucial role in shaping individual behaviors and relationships. Acknowledging and understanding these norms is essential for harmonious interactions.

6.3 Navigating Family Expectations

Family expectations often come with traditions, rituals, and hopes for the future. These can sometimes clash with individual desires and choices, leading to tension within relationships.

6.4 Balancing Autonomy and Family Bonds

Striking a balance between pursuing personal autonomy and honoring familial ties is a delicate task. Open communication is key to aligning personal aspirations with familial expectations.

6.5 Approaches for Navigating Family Expectations

1. Transparent Communication: Openly discuss family expectations, addressing potential conflicts early on.

2. Establishing Boundaries: Set boundaries that protect the relationship while respecting family dynamics.

3. Shared Vision: Create a shared vision of your relationship's future that takes into account both individual and family aspirations.

4. Educating Families: Introduce your partner to your family's cultural norms and values, fostering understanding and acceptance.

5. Prioritizing Respect: Respectfully address differences with family members while maintaining the core respect for cultural values.

6.6 Allies in the Family

Identify family members who might be more open-minded or understanding and involve them as allies who can mediate and advocate for the relationship within the family.

6.7 Fostering an Inclusive Environment

As relationships progress, consider gradually integrating your partner into family gatherings and events, allowing them to experience and participate in traditions.

6.8 Addressing Inter-Cultural Clashes

Clashes between your partner and family might arise due to cultural differences. Address these conflicts promptly and constructively, focusing on mutual respect.

6.9 Seeking Professional Help

In some cases, seeking the guidance of relationship counselors or therapists can provide a safe space for discussing complex family dynamics and expectations.

6.10 Embracing the Blend

Over time, relationships with extended families can evolve into harmonious blends of traditions and values. This process requires patience, adaptability, and mutual understanding.

In conclusion, Chapter 6 delves into the multifaceted world of family and social dynamics in cross-cultural relationships. By recognizing the impact of extended families and societal norms, openly communicating with partners and families, and finding ways to balance personal autonomy with family ties, individuals can navigate these intricacies while nurturing the relationship's growth. This chapter forms the foundation for the subsequent exploration of conflict resolution, intimacy, and long-term relationship sustainability within the ever-evolving context of culturally diverse backgrounds.

7

Balancing Individual Identities

Cross-cultural relationships often require a delicate balance between nurturing the relationship and preserving individual cultural identities. This chapter delves into the challenge of maintaining these identities within a partnership while also exploring strategies to celebrate and integrate both partners' cultural backgrounds.

7.1 The Duality of Identity

Individual identities are deeply intertwined with cultural backgrounds. Balancing these identities while fostering a shared connection poses unique challenges and opportunities.

7.2 The Tension of Assimilation and Preservation

Cultural assimilation, while fostering unity, can sometimes lead to the erasure of individual cultural identities. On the other hand, overly preserving cultural identities might create distance within the partnership.

7.3 The Importance of Individual Identities

Preserving individual identities is vital for self-esteem, self-expression, and overall well-being. These identities are reservoirs of personal history, values, and experiences.

7.4 Strategies for Celebrating and Integrating Cultures

1. Cultural Exchange: Regularly engage in activities from both partners' cultures to foster mutual understanding and appreciation.

2. Festivals and Celebrations: Participate in each other's cultural festivals and celebrations to create shared memories.

3. Language: Incorporate language learning into your journey, enabling you to communicate in both partners' languages.

4. Cuisine: Share and prepare dishes from each other's cultures, indulging in culinary adventures.

5. Art and Creativity: Collaborate on artistic endeavors that showcase the fusion of both cultural influences.

6. Travel: Explore each other's countries, experiencing firsthand the origins of your partner's culture.

7. Family Traditions: Integrate aspects of both partners' family traditions into your shared life.

7.5 Communication about Boundaries

Openly discussing the boundaries of cultural integration is crucial. Both partners should express their comfort levels and areas where they'd like to preserve their cultural identities.

7.6 Embracing the Blend

Strive to create a harmonious blend of cultural identities. This involves weaving elements from both cultures into daily life, creating a unique tapestry.

7.7 Respecting Cultural Differences

Recognize that some aspects of cultural identities might differ, and that's okay. The key is to approach these differences with curiosity and respect.

7.8 Negotiating Decisions with Cultural Context

Cultural backgrounds often influence decision-making approaches. When making significant decisions, consider the cultural context that shapes each partner's perspective.

7.9 Encouraging Growth and Exploration

Support each other in exploring and growing within your respective cultural identities. This can include learning new skills, delving into cultural history, or connecting with like-minded individuals.

7.10 Continual Conversation

Balancing individual identities is an ongoing process. Regular conversations about how both partners feel in terms of identity can help adjust strategies as needed.

In conclusion, Chapter 7 delves into the intricate dance of balancing individual cultural identities within a cross-cultural partnership. By recognizing the importance of maintaining these identities, celebrating and integrating both partners' cultural backgrounds, and fostering open communication about boundaries and comfort levels, individuals can create a relationship that thrives on the strengths of its cultural diversity. This chapter paves the way for the exploration of conflict resolution, intimacy, and long-term relationship sustainability within the context of diverse cultural identities.

8

Overcoming Stereotypes and Misunderstandings

Cultural diversity can sometimes be overshadowed by stereotypes and misconceptions that arise from lack of understanding. This chapter delves into the strategies that individuals can employ to address these challenges, fostering open-mindedness, empathy, and authentic connections.

8.1 The Impact of Stereotypes and Misunderstandings

Stereotypes and misunderstandings can hinder meaningful connections by perpetuating biases and misrepresenting cultural backgrounds.

8.2 Identifying Stereotypes and Biases

Awareness is the first step. Recognizing when stereotypes or biases are at play is crucial for challenging and changing them.

8.3 Strategies for Addressing Stereotypes and Misconceptions

1. Education: Educate yourself about different cultures to challenge existing stereotypes.

2. Self-Reflection: Examine your own biases and preconceptions, fostering a deeper understanding of your reactions.

3. Open Dialogue: Engage in conversations that address stereotypes without defensiveness.

4. Storytelling: Share personal experiences that counter stereotypes, offering nuanced perspectives.

5. Cultural Exchange: Interact with individuals from different cultural backgrounds to gain firsthand insights.

6. Media Literacy: Analyze media portrayals critically to separate stereotypes from reality.

7. Ask Questions: When interacting with someone from a different background, inquire about their experiences and perspectives.

8.4 Fostering Open-Mindedness

1. Curiosity: Approach cultural differences with curiosity rather than judgment.

2. Cultural Humility: Recognize that you might not fully understand another person's experiences or perspectives.

3. Embrace Uncomfortable Conversations: Embrace discomfort as an opportunity for growth and learning.

8.5 Developing Empathy

1. Active Listening: Listen deeply to others' stories and experiences without interrupting or imposing your perspective.

2. Stepping into Others' Shoes: Practice seeing the world from another person's point of view.

3. Shared Humanity: Recognize the shared human experiences that transcend cultural boundaries.

4. Cultural Context: Understand that cultural norms and experiences shape behavior and reactions.

8.6 Challenging Your Own Assumptions

Regularly question your assumptions about others. This practice encourages a more nuanced and empathetic understanding.

8.7 Addressing Misunderstandings Constructively

When misunderstandings occur, approach them with patience, seeking to understand the underlying causes rather than blaming cultural differences.

8.8 Strengthening Relationships through Understanding

Overcoming stereotypes and misunderstandings strengthens relationships, fostering a deep bond based on genuine understanding and respect.

8.9 Role of Vulnerability

Being vulnerable about your own cultural background and experiences can create a safe space for open dialogue and bridge-building.

8.10 Long-Term Commitment

Overcoming stereotypes and misunderstandings is an ongoing commitment. Consistently challenging biases and promoting empathy leads to lasting change.

In conclusion, Chapter 8 addresses the complex issue of overcoming stereotypes and misunderstandings within culturally diverse relationships. By identifying biases, adopting strategies to challenge stereotypes, fostering open-mindedness, and practicing empathy, individuals can transform their perspectives and build connections that transcend surface differences. This chapter lays the groundwork for the exploration of conflict resolution, intimacy, and long-term relationship sustainability within the context of authentically understanding and respecting diverse cultural backgrounds.

9

Navigating Celebrations and Holidays

Celebrations and holidays provide opportunities for individuals in cross-cultural relationships to come together, honor their respective backgrounds, and create new shared traditions. This chapter delves into the art of celebrating holidays and traditions from both partners' cultures, as well as strategies for building new, meaningful shared traditions.

9.1 The Significance of Celebrations and Holidays

Holidays and celebrations hold deep cultural, social, and emotional significance. Acknowledging and embracing these occasions can foster understanding and connection.

9.2 Celebrating Traditions from Both Cultures

1. Open Dialogue: Discuss the significance of holidays and traditions in each culture. Share stories and memories associated with these occasions.

2. Alternate Celebrations: On occasions when both cultures have festivities, explore ways to alternate celebrations from year to year.

3. Combining Elements: Integrate elements from each culture's celebrations into one event, reflecting the diversity of your partnership.

4. Shared Values: Identify shared values and themes that can be woven into celebrations from both cultures.

9.3 Creating Meaningful Shared Traditions

1. Jointly Crafted Rituals: Collaboratively design new rituals that reflect both partners' cultural values and aspirations.

2. Incorporating Personal Touches: Integrate personal experiences, hobbies, or passions into new traditions to make them uniquely yours.

3. Commemorate Significant Moments: Design traditions to celebrate milestones in your relationship's journey.

4. Cultural Exchange Gifts: Exchange gifts that represent each other's cultures, fostering mutual appreciation.

5. Culinary Adventures: Experiment with cooking dishes that blend both partners' culinary traditions.

9.4 Fostering Flexibility

Recognize that not all holidays and traditions can be celebrated with equal fervor. Flexibility allows for a balance that respects both partners' cultural backgrounds.

9.5 Embracing Learning Opportunities

Use celebrations and holidays as opportunities to learn about each other's cultural history, practices, and the stories behind them.

9.6 Involving Families

When possible, involve family members in your cross-cultural celebrations to promote understanding and appreciation.

9.7 Ensuring Comfort

Ensure that celebrations respect both partners' comfort levels and adhere to any religious or cultural requirements.

9.8 Honoring Ancestors and Roots

Celebrate holidays that honor ancestors or cultural heritage to deepen your connection to each other's backgrounds.

9.9 Adapting over Time

As your relationship evolves, your celebration strategies might need to adapt. Remain open to adjusting traditions as needed.

9.10 The Joy of Creating Memories

Remember that the ultimate goal is to create cherished memories and experiences that reflect your shared journey.

In conclusion, Chapter 9 explores the nuanced world of celebrating holidays and traditions in cross-cultural relationships. By appreciating the significance of celebrations, integrating elements from both partners' cultures, and crafting new shared traditions, individuals can honor their diverse backgrounds while building connections that are uniquely their own. This chapter sets the stage for the exploration of conflict resolution, intimacy, and long-term relationship sustainability within the context of shared celebrations that bridge cultures and create lasting memories.

10

Intercultural Parenting

Raising children in an intercultural relationship adds another layer of complexity and opportunity to navigate. This chapter delves into the challenges and rewards of intercultural parenting, exploring how to make decisions, foster understanding, and pass on cultural values within a diverse family unit.

10.1 The Unique Landscape of Intercultural Parenting

Intercultural parenting encompasses the melding of different cultural backgrounds, values, and traditions to shape a cohesive family identity.

10.2 Decision-Making in Parenting

1. Open Communication: Engage in candid discussions about parenting strategies, discipline methods, and cultural values to ensure alignment.

2. Joint Decision-Making: Collaboratively make decisions that honor both

partners' perspectives, finding middle ground where necessary.

3. Respecting Cultural Norms: Acknowledge that different cultures may approach parenting differently, and explore ways to respect these differences.

10.3 Fostering Cultural Understanding in Children

1. Storytelling: Share stories from both partners' backgrounds, helping children understand their heritage and the values it embodies.

2. Cultural Exploration: Introduce children to diverse cultural experiences through literature, music, art, and food.

3. Celebrating Holidays: Embrace holidays and traditions from both cultures, creating a sense of belonging and appreciation.

4. Language Learning: Introduce children to languages spoken in both partners' cultures, enabling them to communicate with extended family.

10.4 Encouraging Open-Mindedness and Empathy

1. Lead by Example: Demonstrate open-mindedness and empathy in your interactions, teaching children the importance of these qualities.

2. Teaching About Diversity: Explain that the world is diverse and that differences are to be celebrated and respected.

3. Foster Curiosity: Encourage children to ask questions about cultural differences, answering with patience and age-appropriate explanations.

10.5 Creating New Family Traditions

1. Blending Cultures: Develop traditions that incorporate elements from

both partners' backgrounds, fostering a sense of unity.

2. Family Rituals: Craft routines that reinforce family bonds, such as weekly meals or outings that integrate both cultures.

10.6 Addressing External Influences

Prepare children for potential challenges they might face outside the home due to their diverse background. Teach them to handle questions and misunderstandings with grace.

10.7 Nurturing Bicultural Identity

Help children develop a bicultural identity that honors both cultures, emphasizing that they don't have to choose one over the other.

10.8 Learning from Each Other

Recognize that parenting in an intercultural relationship is a continual learning experience. Embrace the wisdom and insights both partners bring to the table.

10.9 Supporting Individuality

Acknowledge that your children might choose different aspects from each culture to identify with. Support their choices and celebrate their individuality.

10.10 Unity in Diversity

Ultimately, aim to create an environment where your children feel loved, supported, and empowered to embrace their unique identity in a diverse world.

In conclusion, Chapter 10 delves into the multifaceted world of intercultural parenting. By navigating decision-making, fostering cultural understanding, teaching open-mindedness, creating new traditions, and nurturing a bicultural identity, parents can raise children who appreciate diversity and embody the best of both cultural backgrounds. This chapter lays the groundwork for the exploration of conflict resolution, intimacy, and long-term family sustainability within the context of intercultural parenting that nurtures a vibrant tapestry of values and experiences.

11

Managing Conflicts and Challenges

Cultural differences, while enriching relationships, can also lead to conflicts. This chapter delves into the intricacies of how cultural disparities might trigger disagreements and offers practical tools for resolving conflicts respectfully and constructively within a culturally diverse partnership.

11.1 The Role of Cultural Differences in Conflicts

Cultural backgrounds often shape communication styles, values, and norms, which can become sources of misunderstandings and conflicts.

11.2 Sources of Conflict

1. Miscommunication: Differences in communication styles can lead to misinterpretations and frustrations.

2. Value Clashes: Conflicting cultural values might arise, causing disagree-

ments over parenting, relationships, and more.

3. Family Expectations: Family pressures and expectations, rooted in cultural norms, can create conflicts.

4. Decision-Making Approaches: Disagreements over how decisions are made can arise due to cultural differences.

11.3 Tools for Resolving Conflicts Respectfully

1. Active Listening: Practice attentive listening to understand the root causes of conflicts.

2. Express Feelings: Articulate your feelings and perspective, focusing on "I" statements to avoid sounding accusatory.

3. Cultural Humility: Approach conflicts with humility, acknowledging that your perspective might not be the only valid one.

4. Empathy: Put yourself in the other person's shoes to understand their perspective and emotions.

5. Clarification: Seek clarification when points are unclear, and paraphrase to ensure accurate understanding.

11.4 The Importance of Timing

Choose an appropriate time and place to address conflicts, allowing both partners to be present and focused.

11.5 Avoiding Blame and Stereotypes

Refrain from blaming cultural differences for conflicts. Instead, explore the specific issues and feelings causing the disagreement.

11.6 Seeking Common Ground

Identify shared values or goals that can serve as a foundation for finding solutions.

11.7 Compromise and Flexibility

Work together to find compromises that honor both partners' perspectives and allow for flexibility.

11.8 Third-Party Mediation

If conflicts become challenging to resolve, consider seeking the guidance of a neutral third party, such as a counselor.

11.9 Family Dynamics and Support

In conflicts involving extended families, communicate your needs and boundaries while also involving supportive family members if necessary.

11.10 The Bigger Picture

Remember that conflicts are part of any relationship. Viewing them as opportunities for growth can help build a stronger partnership.

In conclusion, Chapter 11 delves into the complex realm of managing conflicts and challenges within culturally diverse relationships. By understanding the sources of conflicts, adopting tools for respectful resolution, and fostering empathy and flexibility, individuals can navigate disagreements in ways that strengthen the relationship. This chapter lays the groundwork for the exploration of intimacy, long-term relationship sustainability, and personal growth within the context of a partnership that thrives on effective conflict management and understanding.

12

Embracing the Journey

The journey of navigating cultural differences within a relationship is one of growth, learning, and deep connection. This chapter invites individuals to reflect on their experiences, highlights key takeaways, and offers guidance for fostering a strong, resilient, and enriching intercultural relationship.

12.1 The Evolution of Relationships

Acknowledge how your relationship has evolved through the challenges and triumphs of embracing cultural differences.

12.2 Celebrating Growth and Learning

Reflect on the personal growth and insights you've gained as you navigated cultural disparities.

12.3 Embracing Flexibility and Open-Mindedness

Recognize that relationships are a continuous journey of adaptation and openness to change.

12.4 Key Takeaways from the Journey

1. Communication Is Key: Effective communication serves as a cornerstone for understanding and resolving conflicts.

2. Cultural Humility: Approaching your partner's culture with humility fosters mutual respect and appreciation.

3. Shared Values: Identifying shared values and goals strengthens the foundation of your relationship.

4. Empathy and Open-Mindedness: Cultivating these qualities creates a space for understanding and growth.

5. Creating New Traditions: Integrating elements from both cultures into your shared life creates a unique bond.

6. Respecting Individual Identity: Balancing individual and shared identities enriches the partnership.

7. Conflict Resolution: Conflict is natural; the way you navigate it shapes the resilience of your relationship.

12.5 Guidance for a Strong Intercultural Relationship

1. Continuous Learning: Keep learning about each other's cultures and remain curious about your partner's experiences.

2. Celebrate Diversity: View cultural differences as assets that enrich your relationship.

3. Prioritize Connection: Regularly invest time in connecting on both emotional and cultural levels.

4. Communication Rituals: Develop communication rituals that allow you to check in about cultural dynamics and feelings.

5. Flexibility and Adaptability: Be prepared to adapt as your relationship and circumstances evolve.

6. Shared Goals: Continually revisit and update your shared goals to ensure alignment and growth.

7. Nurturing Love and Affection: Express love and appreciation regularly, reinforcing the emotional foundation of your partnership.

12.6 Embracing the Future Together

Approach the future with excitement, knowing that your shared journey will continue to evolve and thrive.

12.7 Recognizing Your Unique Story

Acknowledge that your relationship's narrative is unique, shaped by your personal histories and the cultural tapestries you've woven together.

12.8 Contribution to a Diverse World

Your intercultural relationship contributes to a more inclusive, interconnected world, inspiring others to embrace diversity.

12.9 Embracing the Journey of Lifelong Learning

View your relationship as an ongoing opportunity for growth, learning, and celebration.

12.10 A Strong Foundation for the Future

Remember that the strength of your relationship lies in your willingness to embrace the journey, embrace each other, and embrace the beauty of your unique partnership.

In conclusion, Chapter 12 reflects on the transformative journey of navigating cultural differences within a relationship. By celebrating growth, embracing flexibility, and fostering continuous learning and empathy, individuals can create a strong, resilient intercultural partnership. This chapter encapsulates the essence of the exploration into conflict resolution, intimacy, and long-term relationship sustainability, offering guidance for navigating the challenges and rewards of a relationship that thrives on the power of cultural diversity.

Conclusion: Embracing Cultural Diversity in Relationships

The journey of embracing cultural diversity within relationships is one that unfolds with a tapestry of challenges and triumphs, growth and understanding. This exploration has delved into the intricacies of navigating cultural differences, celebrating traditions, fostering empathy, and building connections that transcend borders and backgrounds. As we conclude this journey, it's important to reinforce the notion that embracing cultural diversity is an ongoing process, rich with opportunities for learning, deepening connections, and personal transformation.

The Ever-Evolving Path

Cultural diversity is a dynamic and evolving landscape. Just as relationships grow and transform, so too do the ways in which we navigate the intersections of cultures. The insights gained from this journey are not finite; they provide a foundation upon which to build, adapt, and thrive in an ever-changing world.

A Journey of Patience and Curiosity

As you traverse the path of an intercultural relationship, remember that patience is your ally. Embrace the fact that understanding and harmonizing cultural differences takes time. Each moment of misunderstanding or challenge is an opportunity for growth and connection.

Approach your partner's cultural background with curiosity, seeking to understand and learn rather than judge. Curiosity fosters open-mindedness, enabling you to see the world from different perspectives and nurturing empathy.

A Willingness to Learn

In an intercultural relationship, the willingness to learn is a powerful asset. Embrace the richness of your partner's culture, and allow it to broaden your horizons. Continually educate yourself about different cultural norms, traditions, and histories, using each lesson as a stepping stone toward a deeper connection.

A World of Possibilities

Your intercultural relationship has the potential to contribute to a world where diversity is celebrated, connections are nurtured, and understanding flourishes. By fostering these values within your partnership, you become ambassadors of change, shaping a world that values and embraces the beauty of cultural differences.

A Lifelong Journey

Remember that the journey of navigating cultural diversity is lifelong. Just as cultures are multifaceted and ever-changing, so too are relationships. Embrace the challenges, celebrate the victories, and approach each moment with the knowledge that you're on a path of continuous growth, exploration, and love.

As you move forward, know that the insights gained from this journey will guide you through the complexities of conflict, intimacy, and the long-term sustainability of your relationship. Embrace your journey with open hearts, open minds, and an enduring commitment to learning, understanding, and cherishing the diversity that brings you together.